A Character Building Book™

Learning About Love from the Life of
Mother Teresa

Brenn Jones

The Rosen Publishing Group's
PowerKids Press™

To the Wiltenburg family

Published in 2002 by The Rosen Publishing Group, Inc.
29 East 21st Street, New York, NY 10010

First Edition

Book Design: Michael Caroleo

Project Editor: Emily Raabe

Photo Credits: p. 4, 15 © Patsy Lynch/CORBIS; p.8, 19 © Associated Press AP; p. 11 © Earl & Nazima Kowall/CORBIS; p.12 © Alison Wright/CORBIS; p. 7 16, 20 © Bettmann/CORBIS.

Jones, Brenn
    Learning about love from the life of Mother Teresa. / Brenn Jones. – 1st ed.
        p. cm.
    Includes index.
    ISBN 0-8239-5777-2
    1. Teresa, Mother, 1910- 2. Missionaries of Charity—Biography. 3. Nuns—India—Calcutta—Biography. I. Title.
BX4406.5.Z8 J66 2002
271'.97.—dc21

                                                                                    00-011989
                                                                                    CIP

Manufactured in the United States of America

Contents

Mother Teresa

Mother Teresa was a **nun** in the Catholic Church. She was known around the world because she devoted her life to helping the poorest of the poor. Mother Teresa lived her whole life in **poverty** with the poor people that she helped.

Mother Teresa was born on August 26, 1910, in Skopje, a city in the southern European country of Macedonia. She died in India on September 5, 1997. In her 87 years of life, Mother Teresa brought love to millions of people.

◀ *Like the famous Indian leader Mahatma Gandhi, Mother Teresa believed that a person "who serves the poor, serves God."*

Growing Up

Mother Teresa was born Agnes Gonxha Bojaxhiu. Agnes' father died when she was very young. When she was twelve years old, Agnes decided that she wanted to be a nun. When she turned 18, she left her home and went to Ireland for her **religious** training. At the **convent** in Ireland, Agnes dedicated herself to God. "I am like a pencil in his hand," she said. She meant by this that God would be in charge of the rest of her life. Agnes changed her name to Teresa in honor of the French saint Therese of Lisieux.

This maps shows Ireland, with an image of Mother Theresa praying in the background. ▶

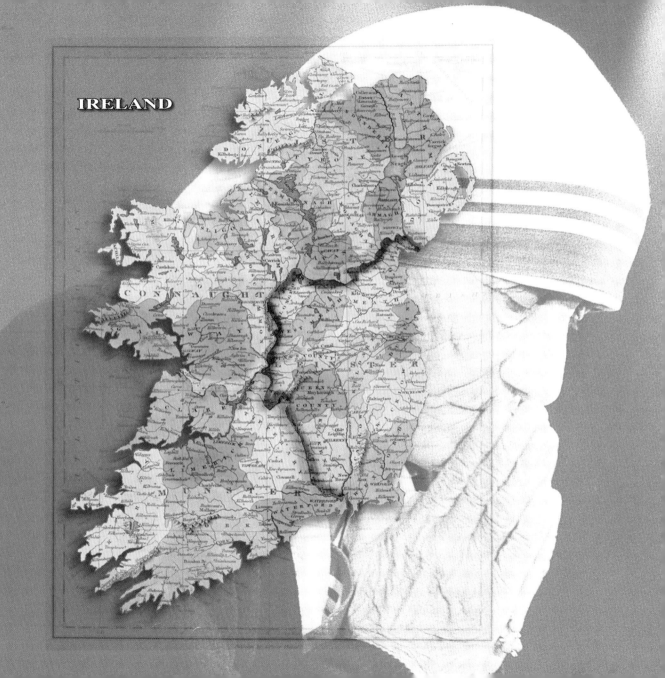

IRELAND

The Missionaries of Charity

In 1929, the Catholic Church sent Mother Teresa to teach at a high school in Calcutta, India. Mother Teresa taught at the high school for seventeen years, but she wanted to work more closely with poor people. She asked the **Vatican** to let her start a center for poor people in Calcutta. In 1950, the Vatican allowed Mother Teresa to start the Missionaries of Charity. Nuns who joined the mission had to **vow**, or promise, that they would spend their lives taking care of the poor and the needy.

◀ *This is Mother Teresa and some of the other nuns who belong to the Missionaries of Charity.*

Calcutta

Calcutta is one of the most crowded cities in the world. Over twelve million people live there. Per square mile, Calcutta is almost five times as crowded as New York City.

Many people in Calcutta do not have enough food and clean water to stay healthy. Some don't even have homes. These people live in the streets. The streets are full of garbage, and the people who live there often get sick. Mother Teresa decided that the Missionaries of Charity would help the poorest and the sickest people of Calcutta.

More than 30% of the people in Calcutta live in poor areas. These areas, called slums, are often filled with garbage. ▶

Pure Heart

One day while she was walking in Calcutta, Mother Teresa found a sick woman lying on the street. Mother Teresa took the woman to a nearby hospital but the hospital refused to treat her. Mother Teresa wanted this woman and other sick and dying people to feel loved. In 1952, she opened the Nirmal Hriday (Pure Heart) Home for the Dying in Kalighat, a neighborhood in southern Calcutta. Since then, Mother Teresa and those who work at the Home have rescued 54,000 sick people from the streets of Calcutta.

◀ *Since it opened, 23,000 people have died in peace at the Home for the Dying in Kalighat.*

Living Simply

In order to help the poorest people Mother Teresa believed that she must be poor. Mother Teresa did not have money. She did not have a car, or a television, or a computer. "The less you have, the more free you are," she said. "Poverty for us is a freedom."

Mother Teresa always wore the same thing. She wore a simple white cotton **sari** with blue stripes. She pinned a small **crucifix** on the left shoulder of the sari. The crucifix **symbolized** Mother Teresa's love for God.

In this picture, you can see the blue stripes on Mother Teresa's sari, and the small crucifix on her left shoulder. ▶

Nobel Peace Prize

In 1979, Mother Teresa won the Nobel Peace Prize. The Nobel Peace Prize is given each year to a person who has worked for peace in the world. There is always a fancy **banquet** for the winner. Mother Teresa requested that her banquet be canceled. She wanted the money for the banquet to be used to feed the poor instead. The people in charge of the banquet canceled it for Mother Teresa. Mother Teresa used the $7,000 that was for the banquet to hold a dinner for 2,000 poor people on Christmas day.

Mother Teresa won many awards for her work. In this photograph, taken in 1971, Pope Paul VI is presenting her with the Pope John XXIII Peace Prize.

A Worldwide Mission

Other nuns wanted to help Mother Teresa. With more helping hands, the Missionaries of Charity opened branches around the world. In 1964, Mother Teresa and a nun named Sister Nirmala opened a Missionaries of Charity Center in the South American country of Venezuela. The Missionaries of Charity opened their first United States center in New York City. There are now 80 Missionary **Brothers** of Charity as well. The brothers, like the nuns, devote their lives to helping the poor and the sick.

Today, 4,000 sisters, all wearing simple white cotton saris, ▶
work at 500 missions in over 100 countries around the world.

A New Challenge

The Missionaries of Charity have built schools, **orphanages**, and **refuges** for sick people and old people all around the world.

Recently a terrible new disease has come to India. This disease is the **Acquired Immune Deficiency Syndrome**, or AIDS. AIDS is a disease for which there is no cure. Many doctors in India have been afraid to treat AIDS patients. The Missionaries of Charity built some of the first homes for AIDS victims in India. The Missionaries also built homes for AIDS patients in the United States.

◀ *Mother Teresa opened many orphanages around the world. This is Mother Teresa holding a child from one of her orphanages.*

The Saint of the Gutters

Mother Teresa was often called the "Saint of the Gutters" because she was not afraid to go to the poor parts of cities. When Mother Teresa died in 1997, Jacques Chirac, the President of France, said "This evening, there is less love, less **compassion**, less light in the world."

Sister Nirmala has taken over as the leader of the Missionaries of Charity. Under her leadership, the organization continues to spread the love of Mother Teresa.

Glossary

Acquired Immune Deficiency Syndrome (uh-KWIR-ed ih-MYOON di-fi-SHUN-se SIN-drohm) A very serious illness that damages the body's ability to protect itself.

banquet (BAAN-kwet) A large meal eaten in honor of a holiday or special event.

brothers (BRUH-thers) Men who belong to a religious order.

compassion (kum-PA-shin) Kindness toward others.

convent (KON-vent) A place where nuns live.

crucifix (KROO-suh-fiks) A statue of Jesus Christ on the cross.

nun (NUN) A woman who belongs to a religious order.

orphanages (OR-fe-nij-es) Places where orphans live.

poverty (POV-er-tee) Being poor.

refuges (REF-yoo-jes) Shelters from danger.

religious (ri-LIJ-us) Having to do with a religion.

sari (SAR-ee) A piece of clothing worn over the head and shoulder.

symbolized (SIM-buh-lyzed) To have stood for something.

Vatican (VAT-i-ken) The headquarters of the Catholic Church.

vow (VOW) A very important promise.

Index

Web Sites

To learn about Mother Teresa, check out these Web sites:
http://www.tisv.be/mt/life.htm
http://www.cnn.com/world/9709/mother.teresa